The Complete Guitar Player Blues Songbook

by Arthur Dick.

D1612275

Wise Publications
London/New York/Sydney

5-95

Exclusive Distributors:
Music Sales Limited
8/9 Frith Street, London W1V 5TZ, England.
Music Sales Pty Limited
120 Rothschild Avenue, Rosebery, NSW 2018, Australia.

This book © Copyright 1992 by Wise Publications
Order No. AM84484
ISBN 0-7119-2620-4

Compiled by Peter Evans
Arranged by Arthur Dick
Music processed by Musicprint

Music Sales' complete catalogue lists thousands of
titles and is free from your local music shop, or direct from
Music Sales Limited. Please send a cheque/postal order for £1.50 for postage to:
Music Sales Limited, Newmarket Road, Bury St. Edmunds, Suffolk IP33 3YB.

Your Guarantee of Quality
As publishers, we strive to produce every book to the highest
commercial standards.
The music has been freshly engraved and the book has been carefully
designed to minimise awkward page turns and to make playing from it
a real pleasure.
Particular care has been given to specifying acid-free, neutral-sized
paper which has not been elemental chlorine bleached but produced with
special regard for the environment. Throughout, the printing and
binding have been planned to ensure a sturdy, attractive
publication which should give years of enjoyment.
If your copy fails to meet our high standards, please inform us and
we will gladly replace it.

Unauthorised reproduction of any part of
this publication by any means including photocopying is
an infringement of copyright.

Printed in the United Kingdom by
J.B. Offset Printers (Marks Tey) Limited, Marks Tey, Essex.

Crossroads Blues   Words & Music by Robert Johnson.

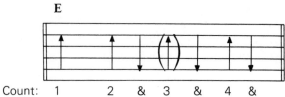

4/4 Rhythm/Strumming
See Course Book No. 1 Pages 12-14

Count: 1   2 & 3 & 4 &

I went to the cross - road ____ fell down on my knee ____

____ I went to the cross - road ____

fell down on my knee ____ I asked the Lord to have

mer - cy "Save poor Bob if you please". ____

Stand - in' at the ____

Verse 2:
Standing at the crossroad,
I tried to flag a ride
Standing at the crossroad
I tried to flag a ride
Didn't nobody seem to know me
Everybody passed me by.

Verse 3:
The sun going down, boy,
Dark gonna catch me here
The sun going down, boy,
Dark gonna catch me here
I haven't got no loving sweet woman
That loves and feels my care.

Verse 4:
You can run, you can run,
Tell my friend, poor Willie Brown,
You can run, you can run,
Tell my friend, poor Willie Brown,
Lord, that I'm standing at the crossroad
Babe, I believe I'm sinking down.

© Copyright 1992 Dorsey Brothers Music Limited,
8/9 Frith Street, London W1.
All Rights Reserved. International Copyright Secured.

Walkin' Blues

Words & Music by Robert Johnson.

4/4 Rhythm/Strumming
See Course Book No. 1 Pages 12-14

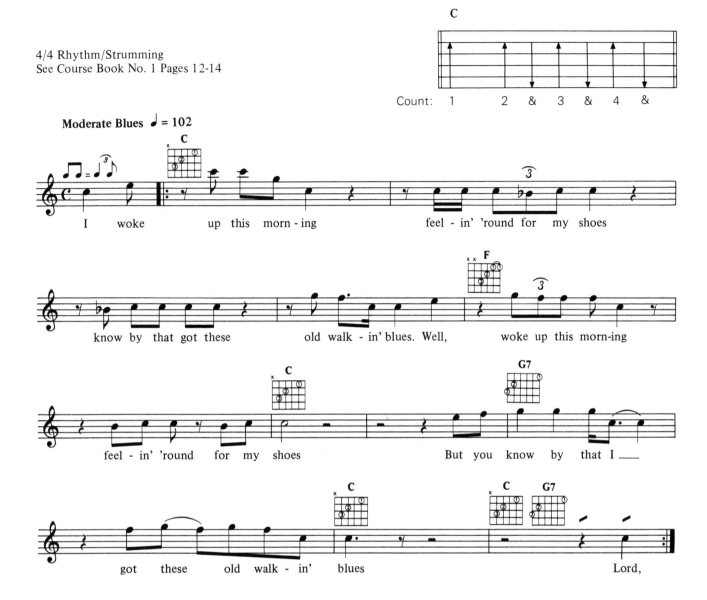

Moderate Blues ♩ = 102

I woke up this morn-ing feel-in' 'round for my shoes know by that got these old walk-in' blues. Well, woke up this morn-ing feel-in' 'round for my shoes But you know by that I ___ got these old walk-in' blues Lord,

Verse 2:
Lord, I feel like blowing my old lonesome horn,
Got up this morning my little Bernice was gone
Lord, I feel like blowing my lonesome horn,
Well, I got up this morning, all I had was gone.

Verse 3:
Well, leave this morning if I have to, oh, ride the blinds,
I feel mistreated and I don't mind dyin',
Leavin' this morning, I have to ride the blinds,
Babe, I've been mistreated, baby, and I don't mind dyin'.

Verse 4:
Well, some people tell me that the worried blues ain't bad,
Worst old feeling I most ever had,
Some people tell me that these old worried old blues ain't bad
It's the worst old feeling I most ever had.

Verse 5:
She's got an Elgin movement from her head down to her toes,
Break in on a dollar most anywhere she goes,
Uumh, her head down to her toes,
Lord, she break in on a dollar most everywhere she goes.

© Copyright 1992 Dorsey Brothers Music Limited,
8/9 Frith Street, London W1.
All Rights Reserved. International Copyright Secured.

Need Your Love So Bad Words & Music by Mertis John Jr.

6/8 Rhythm/Bass-strum
See Course Book No. 1 Pages 14-17

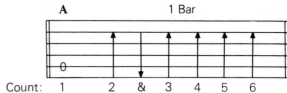

© Copyright 1965 Fort Knox Music Company Incorporated, USA.
Lark Music Limited, Iron Bridge House, 3 Bridge Approach,
London NW1.
All Rights Reserved. International Copyright Secured.

Book 1

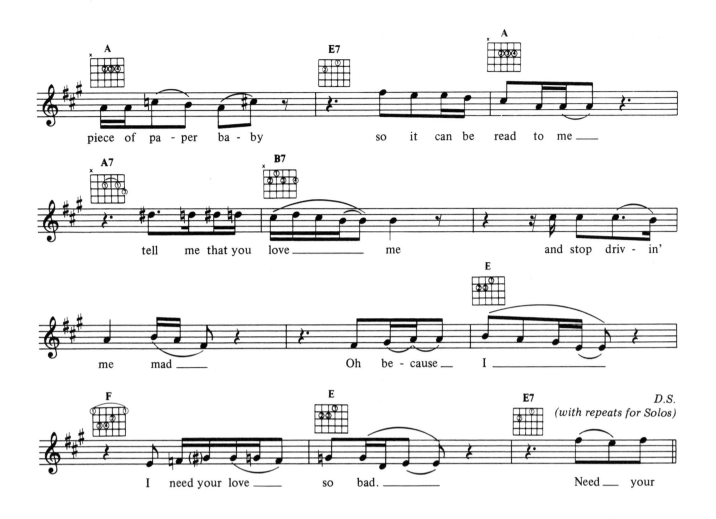

Verse 2:
I need your lips, to feel next to mine
I need someone to stand up, and tell me when I'm lyin'.
And when the lights are low and it's time to go
That's when I need your love so bad.

Verse 3 on S.
Need your soft voice, to talk to me at night
I don't want you to worry baby, I know we can make everything alright.
Listen to my plea baby, bring it to me
Because I need your love so bad.

Madison Blues   Words & Music by Elmore James.

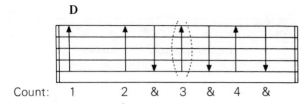

4/4 Rhythm/Strumming/Stress 2nd up-stroke
See Course Book No. 1 Page 12

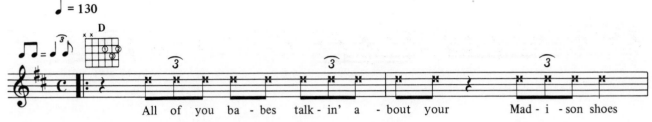

All of you ba - bes talk - in' a - bout your   Mad - i - son shoes

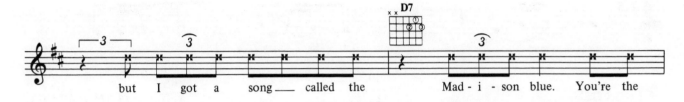

but   I   got   a   song ___ called the   Mad - i - son blue.   You're the

Mad - i - son   blue ___   you're the   Mad - i - son blues ___

we   got   the   Mad - i - son   blues ___

Repeat for sax solo
and verse 2 to Fade

and   walk   a - way   your   shoes.

Verse 2:
I know a girl, her name is Lindyloo
She told me she loved me but I know it ain't true.
Put on your Madison Blues (shoes)
Put on your Madison Blues (shoes)
I got the Madison Blues
Now put on your Madison Blues shoes.

© Copyright 1968 Arc Music Corporation, USA.
Tristan Music Limited, 22 Denmark Street, London WC2.
All Rights Reserved. International Copyright Secured.

The Sky Is Crying

Words & Music by Elmore James & M. Robinson.

12/8 Rhythm/Simple Arpeggio pattern.
See Course Book No. 1 Page 30

Verse 2:
I saw my baby early one mornin'
And she was walkin' on down the street.
I saw my baby early one mornin'
And she was walkin' on down the street.
You know it hurt me so bad, yeah,
It made my poor heart skip a beat.

Verse 3:
I got a bad feelin'
My baby don't love me no more.
I got real bad, bad feelin'
My baby don't love me no more.
You know the sky is cryin', yeah
The tears are rollin' down my nose.

© Copyright 1960 Arc Music Corporation, USA. Warner Chappell
Music Limited, 129 Park Street, London W1.
All Rights Reserved. International Copyright Secured.

Key To The Highway

Words & Music by Big Bill Broonzy & Chas. Segar.

12/8 Rhythm/Swing
See Course Book No. 2 Page 5

Verse 2:
I'm goin' back to the border
Woman where I'm better known
'Cause you haven't done nothin'
Drove a good man away from home.

Verse 3:
As the moon peeks over the mountains
I'll be on my way
I'm gonna roam this old highway
Until the break of day.

Verse 4:
Now give me one, one more kiss baby
Yeah before I go
'Cause I'm gonna leave you running
Walkin' is much too slow.

Verse 5:
So long, so long baby,
Yeah, I must say goodbye
You know I'm gonna roam the highway
Until the day I die.

© Copyright 1941 & 1963 Duchess Music Corporation, USA.
MCA Music Limited, 77 Fulham Palace Road, London W6.
All Rights Reserved. International Copyright Secured.

Whiskey Blues
Words & Music by Luke Jordan.

4/4 Rhythm/Swing/Alternating thumb
See Course Book No. 2 Page 23

Moderate 12/8, swing feel

Well I been ___ sit - tin' here drink - in' ___

I'm just as lone-some as a man can be. ___

Well I be - en

sit - tin' here drink - in' ___

I'm just as lone - some as a man ___ can be. ___

Well now you know that clear-ly you need a wo-man for eve-ry man

I won-der why you don't want ___ for me. ___

*Play Fig. A
as above*

*Repeat for Verse and
Instrumental Fade*

So ma - ny

Verse 2:
So many times.
I told you I wasn't going that far.
So many times.
I told you I wasn't going that far.
Well you know that I've got to drink with my partner.
Stay all night keepin' on out of work.

Verse 3:
Whiskey you ain't no good,
I declare I'm through with you.
Whiskey you ain't no good,
I declare I'm through with you.
You have taken all my money
You have taken my baby too.

© Copyright 1952 by Peer International Corporation, USA.
Southern Music Publishing Company Limited, 8 Denmark Street,
London WC2.
All Rights Reserved. International Copyright Secured.

Steady Rollin' Man

Words & Music by Robert Johnson. Arranged by Eric Clapton.

Book 2

4/4 Rhythm/Alternating thumb
See Course Book No. 2 Pages 23 & 26

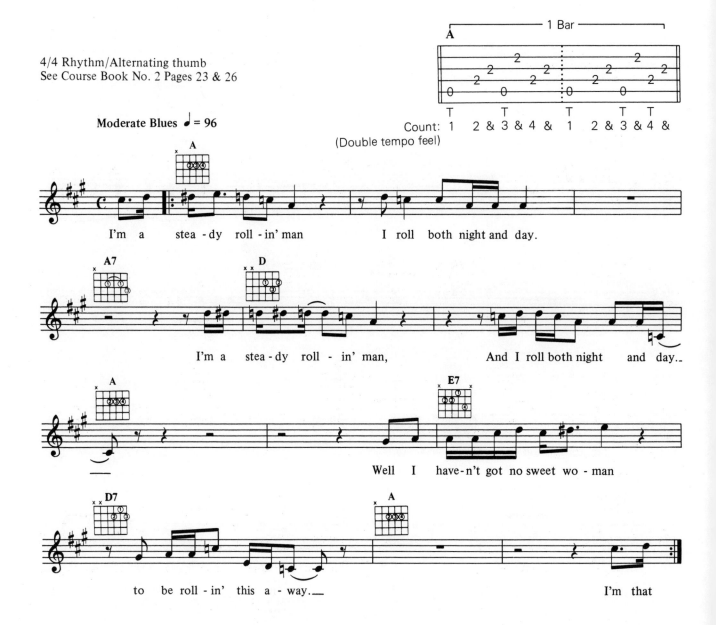

Moderate Blues ♩ = 96

Count: 1   2 & 3 & 4 &   1   2 & 3 & 4 &
(Double tempo feel)

I'm a stea-dy roll-in' man   I roll both night and day.

I'm a stea-dy roll-in' man,   And I roll both night   and day..

Well I have-n't got no sweet wo-man

to be roll-in' this a-way.___   I'm that

Verse 2:
I'm that man that rolls
When icicle's hanging on the tree,
I'm the man that rolls
When icicle's hanging on the tree,
And now you hear me howling, baby,
(Uumh), down on my bended knee.

Verse 3:
I'm a hard working man,
Have been for many years I know,
I'm a hard working man,
Have been for many long years I know,
And some cream puff's using my money,
(Uumh), well, babe, but that'll never be no more.

Verse 4:
You can't give your sweet woman
Everything she wants in one time,
You can't give your sweet woman
Everything she wants in one time
Well, boys, she gets rambling in her brain
(Uumh) some other man on her mind.

Verse 5:
I'm a steady rollin' man,
I roll both night and day,
I am your steady rollin' man
And I roll both night and day
Well I don't have no sweet woman
To be rollin' this a-way.

© Copyright 1974 & 1992 Eric Clapton.
All Rights Reserved. International Copyright Secured.

Sitting On Top Of The World

Words & Music by Chester Burnette.

4/4 Rhythm/Strumming/Swing
See Course Book No. 2 Page 5

Slow Blues ♩ = 64

One sum-mer day _____ She went a-way _____ She'd gone and left me _____ she'd gone to stay _____ but now she's gone _____ and I don't wor-ry._____ _____ 'cos I'm sit-tin' on _____ top of the world._____

Repeat Solos and Verses to Fade

Worked all the

Verse 2:
Worked all the summer
And worked on this farm.
I had to take my Christmas
In my overalls.
But now she's gone, and I don't worry,
'Cos I'm sittin' on top of the world.

Verse 3:
Going down to the freight yard
Just to meet a freight train.
I'm going to leave this town,
Work has done got too hard.
But now she's gone, and I don't worry,
Because I'm sittin' on top of the world.

Verse 4:
As verse 1.

© Copyright 1958 (renewed) Arc Music Corporation, USA.
Tristan Music Limited, 22 Denmark Street, London WC2.
All Rights Reserved. International Copyright Secured.

People Get Ready

Book 2

Words & Music by Curtis Mayfield.

4/4 Rhythm/Alternating thumb
See Course Book No. 2 Page 23

CAPO 1st FRET

Count double time: 1 2 & 3 & 4 & 1 2 & 3 & 4 &

Peo -ple get rea -dy___ there's a train a - com - in'

Don't need___ no bag - gage___ you just

get on___ board.___ All you need is faith___

to hear the die - sel hum - min' Don't

need___ no ti - cket you just thank the Lord.___

Chorus A

B Peo -ple get rea - dy

Harmonica Cue:

To Coda only

On his Peo -ple get rea - dy.

© Copyright 1965 Chi' Sounds/Warner Tamerlane Publishing
Corporation, USA.
Warner Chappell Music Limited, 129 Park Street, London W1.
All Rights Reserved. International Copyright Secured.

14

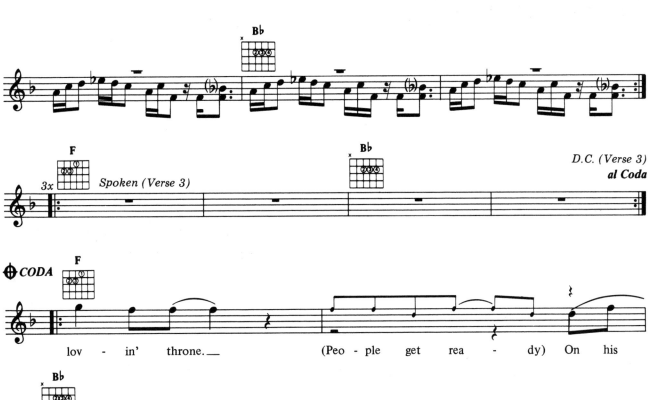

Verse 2:
People get ready, for the train to Jordan
Pickin' up passengers, from coast to coast
Faith is the key, open the door and board her
'Cos there's hope for all, among his loving more.

Chorus B:
People get ready, people get ready
People get ready, people get ready.

Verse 3: Spoken
People, please get ready by the train of love
It doesn't cost you anything,
All you do is get on board
The only giving is giving yourself
This is the last go round
And if you miss the train, I want you to know
You've only got yourself to blame
Me and old Sonny are takin' the same ride
And door's open wide for you, for you.

Verse 3:
There ain't no room, for the hopeless sinner
Who'd hurt all mankind, just to save his own
Have pity on those, whose chances grow slimmer
For there's no hiding place, there's no hiding place.

Chorus B:
There's no hiding place, there's no hiding place.

Coda:
On his loving throne, (people get ready)
On his loving throne, (people get ready)
People get ready, (people get ready)
On a train to Jordan (people get ready)
It's pickin' up passengers (people get ready)
From coast to coast (people get ready)
Faith is the key (people get ready)
Open the door (people get ready).

Cockroach

Words & Music by Betty Crotcher & Willia Deannie Parker.

© Copyright Irving Music Incorporated, USA.
Rondor Music (London) Limited, 10a Parsons Green, London SW6.
All Rights Reserved. International Copyright Secured.

Verse 2:
You said you'd cook my breakfast
You'd bring it to the bed,
And if I feel bad now
You'll be there to rub my achin' head;
Here I am,
I'm wrapped up in love again
Yeah, you say you don't want to marry me,
Little girl you just wanna be my friend.

Verse 3:
Won't be no use to callin' me
Won't answer the phone,
I'll have someone to tell you little girl
That I'm not at home;
Here I am,
I'm wrapped up in love again
Yeah, you say you don't want to marry me
Little girl you just wanna be my friend.

Ad lib vocals:
Now come on woman,
I want you to love me
Come on baby
You got a right to love me . . .

On The Road Again

Words & Music by Allen Wilson & Floyd Jones.

4/4 Rhythm/Slight swing
See Course Book No. 2 Page 6

Moderate Blues ♩ = 124

Well I'm so _____ tired of cry - in' but I'm out _____

_____ on the road _____ a - gain, I'm on the road a - gain _____

Well I'm so _____ tired of cry - in' but I'm out _____

_____ on the road _____ a - gain I'm on the road a - gain. _____

_____ I ain't got _____ no wo - man just to

1, 2.

call my spe - cial friend. _____

© Copyright 1968 EMI Catalogue Partnership/EMI Unart Catalog
Incorporated/Lawn Music Company, USA.
EMI United Partnership Limited, 127 Charing Cross Road, London WC2.
All Rights Reserved. International Copyright Secured.

You know the

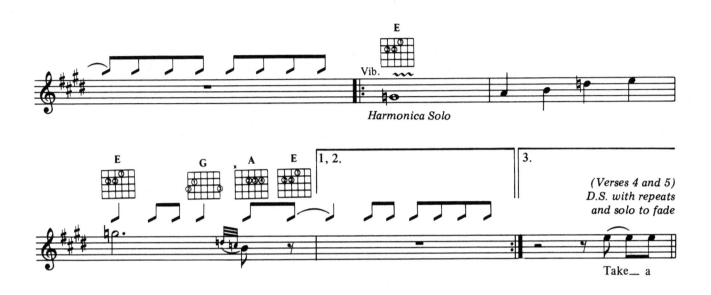

Harmonica Solo

(Verses 4 and 5)
D.S. with repeats
and solo to fade

Take__ a

Verse 2:
You know the first time I travelled, out,
In the rain and snow; in the rain and snow.
You know the first time I travelled, out,
In the rain and snow; in the rain and snow.
I didn't have no fair road, not even no place to go.

Verse 3:
And my dear mother left me, when,
I was quite young; when I was quite young.
And my dear mother left me, when,
I was quite young; when I was quite young.
She said "Lord have mercy, on my wicked son".

Verse 4 on S.
Take a hint from your mama, please,
Don't you cry no more; don't you cry no more.
Take a hint from your mama, please,
Don't you cry no more; don't you cry no more.
'Cos it's soon one mornin', down the road I'm goin'.

Verse 5:
But I ain't goin' down there,
Long old lonesome road; all by myself.
But I ain't goin' down there,
Long old lonesome road; all by myself.
I can't carry you baby, going to carry somebody else.

Ice Cream Man

Words & Music by John Bram.

4/4 Rhythm/Bass-strum/Swing
See Course Book No. 3 Page 14

Moderate Blues ♩ = 126

Sum-mer-time is here need some-thing to keep you cool.

Now sum-mer-time is here need

some-thing to keep you cool. Hey

lit-tle girl I've got-ta song for you.

I'm your ice-cream man par-don me when I'm pass-in' by.

I'm your ice-cream man

Stop me when I'm pass-in' by. I'll

© Copyright 1968 Arc Music Corporation, USA.
Tristan Music Limited, 22 Denmark Street, London WC2.
All Rights Reserved. International Copyright Secured.

cool you off — lit - tle girl   I   gua - ran -tee I sa - tis -fy. —

I   got green sa - lad juice   Dix - ie   cup

Pop - si - cle   and push - ups too. I'm your ice - cream man

Stop   me when I'm pass - in'   by. —   I'll —

cool you off — lit - tle girl   I   gua - ran - tee I sa - tis - fy. —

Verse 4 (D.C.)
I knew you'd come along
Just about seven o'clock
I knew you'd come along
Just about seven o'clock
Now if you let me cool you off this time
You'd be my regular star.

Verse 5:
I got all flavours
Including pineapple too
I got all flavours
Including pineapple too
Now one of my flavours little girl
Gotta be just right for you.

Canned Heat Blues

Words & Music by Tommy Johnson.

Book 3

4/4 Rhythm/Arpeggio/Swing
See Course Book No. 3 Pages 17-19

Moderate Blues ♩ = 112

Cry-ing, canned heat__ canned heat ma-ma, Cry-ing sure, Lord__ kill-ing

me. Cry-ing canned heat__ ma-ma, Sure Lord,__ kill-ing

me. Takes_____ al-co-rut to

take those canned heat blues.__ Cry-ing,

Verse 2:
Crying, mama, mama, mama, you know, canned heat killing me.
Crying, mama, mama, mama, crying, canned heat is killing me.
Canned heat don't kill me, crying, babe, I'll never die.

Verse 3:
I woked up, up this morning, with canned heat on my mind.
Woked up this morning, canned heat was on my mind.
Woked up this morning with canned heat, Lord, on my mind.

Verse 4:
Crying, Lord, Lord, I wonder, canned heat, Lord, killing me.
Takes alcorut, baby, satisfy my soul.
Take a brownskin woman, Lord, do the easy roll.

Verse 5:
I woked up, up this morning, crying, canned heat 'round my bed.
Run here, somebody, take these canned heat blues.
Run here, somebody, and take these canned heat blues.

Verse 6:
Crying, mama, mama, mama, crying, canned heat killing me.
Believe to my soul, Lord, it gonna kill me dead.

© Copyright Peer International Corporation, USA.
Southern Music Publishing Company Limited, 8 Denmark Street,
London WC2.
All Rights Reserved. International Copyright Secured.

Talk To Me Baby

Words & Music by Willie Dixon.

4/4 Rhythm/Bass-strum
See Course Book No. 3 Page 11

Count: 1   2 & 3 & 4 &

Moderate Blues ♩ = 112

I just talked to my ba - by on the te - le - phone (she said)

Stop what you're do-in' and come on home__ I can't hold out,

I can't hold out __ too long. _____ I __ get a

real good feel - ing talk - in' to you on __ the

Last time

phone. She said

Verse 2:
She said baby don't you worry
You're my desire
I love you pretty baby
And I hate to see you cry
I can't hold out
I can't hold out too long
I get a real good feelin'
Talkin' to you on the phone.

Verse 3:
She said daddy you can run
Walk or fly
You know I love you baby
You're my heart's desire.
I can't hold out,
I can't hold out too long
I get a real good feelin'
Talkin' to you on the phone.

© Copyright 1968 Arc Music Corporation, USA.
Tristan Music Limited, 22 Denmark Street, London WC2.
All Rights Reserved. International Copyright Secured.

I Ain't Superstitious

Words & Music by Willie Dixon.

Book 3

24 © Copyright 1963 Arc Music Corporation, USA.
Tristan Music Limited, 22 Denmark Street, London WC2.
All Rights Reserved. International Copyright Secured.

Verse 2:
Well my right hand's itchy
I gets some money for sure.
Well my right hand's itchy
I gets some money for sure.
But when I left that job
Somebody got to go.

Verse 3:
As verse 1

Verse 4:
Well the dogs all howling
All over the neighbourhood.
Well the dogs all howl
All over the neighbourhood.
That's a true sign
Things ain't no good.

Verse 5:
As verse 1

Black Magic Woman

Words & Music by Peter Green.

Book 3

4/4 Rhythm/Syncopated arpeggio
See Course Book No. 3 Page 16

[Tune 6th string to D]

Bright feel ♩ = 128

Got a black ma-gic wo-man___ got a black ma-gic wo-man___ yes___ I got-ta black ma-gic wo-man___ got me so blind I can't___ see ___ that she's a black ma-gic wo-man and she's tryin' to make a de-vil out of me.

Don't turn your back on me

Solo Gtr.

bend   reverse bend

© Copyright 1968 King Music Publishing Company Limited.
© Copyright 1970 Bourne-King for United Kingdom and Eire.
© Copyright 1970 Bourne Music Limited, 34-36 Maddox Street,
London W1 for the rest of the World.
All Rights Reserved. International Copyright Secured.

Verse 2:
Don't turn your back on me baby,
Don't turn your back on me baby,
Yes don't turn your back on me baby,
You're messin' around with your tricks.
Don't turn your back on me baby
'Cos you might just break up our magic stick.

Verse 3 on S.
You got your spell on me baby,
You got your spell on me baby,
Yes you got your spell on me baby,
Turnin' my heart into stone.
I need you so bad
Magic woman I can't leave you alone.

Ad lib vocals:
Yes, I need you so bad
I need you darlin'
Yeh I need you darlin'
Yes I want you to love me
I want you to love me . . . etc.

Highway 49 Blues   Words & Music by Big Joe Williams.

4/4 Rhythm/Bass-strum/Swing
See Course Book No. 3 Page 10

Count: 1 & 2 & 3 & 4 &

Moderate blues ♩ = 124

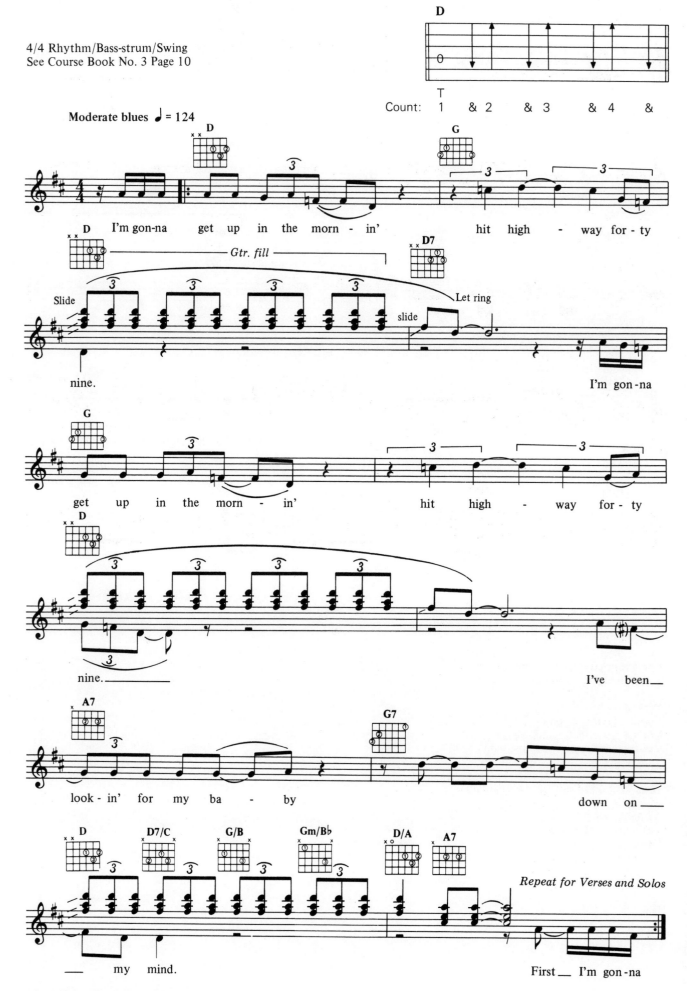

© Copyright 1949 Wabash Music, USA.
MCA Music Limited, 77 Fulham Palace Road, London W6.
All Rights Reserved. International Copyright Secured.

Verse 2:
First I'm gonna stop at the whiskey store
I'm gonna buy me a jug of wine.
First I'm gonna stop at the whiskey store
I'm gonna buy me a jug of wine.
I'm gonna hit the highway
They call highway 49.

Verse 3:
It'll be soon in the mornin'
When I go rollin' in Jacksontown
It'll be soon in the mornin'
When I go rollin' in Jacksontown.
I'll be lookin' for Bonny! My old Bonny
You say she can't be found.

Verse 4:
Bonny my sweet woman
You know she stays on my mind,
Bonny my sweet woman
You know she stays on my mind.
If I can't find that woman
I'm gonna set out and drink my wine.

Spoonful
Words & Music by Willie Dixon.

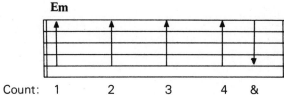

4/4 Rhythm/Slight swing/ Damped strings
See Course Book No. 4 Page 11

Moderate blues shuffle ♩ = 116

It could fill a spoon-ful of dia-monds could fill a spoon-ful of gold___ Just a ___ lit-tle spoon of your___ pre-cious love ___ sa-tis-fy___ my soul ___ Men ___ lies ___ a-bout it; some of them cries ___ a-bout it some of them dies ___ a-bout it Eve-ry-thing's a fight-in' a-bout the spoon-ful___ That

© Copyright 1960 Arc Music Corporation & Hoochie Coochie Music,
USA. Jewel Music Publishing Company Limited, 129 Park Street,
London W1.
All Rights Reserved. International Copyright Secured.

spoon, that spoon, that spoon - ful.___ That spoon, that spoon, that spoon - ful.___ That

spoon, that spoon, that spoon - ful.___ That spoon, that spoon, that

spoon - ful.___

Repeat for Verses
and Solos to Fade

Verse 2:
Could fill a spoon's full of coffee
Could fill a spoon's full of tea
Just a little spoon of your precious love
Is that enough for me?
Men lies about it
Some of them cries about it
Some of them dies about it
Everything's a-fightin' about the spoonful
That spoon, that spoon, that spoonful
That spoon, that spoon, that spoonful
That spoon, that spoon, that spoonful
That spoon, that spoon, that spoonful.

Verse 3:
Could you fill a spoon's full of water
Saved them from the desert sands
Was a little spoon of your love, baby
Saved you from another man.
Men lies about it
Some of them cries about it
Some of them dies about it
Everything's a-fightin' about the spoonful
That spoon, that spoon, that spoonful . . . etc.

Ramblin' On My Mind

Words & Music by Robert Johnson. Arranged by Eric Clapton.

4/4 Rhythm/Blues with embellishments
See Course Book No. 4 Pages 4 & 17-19

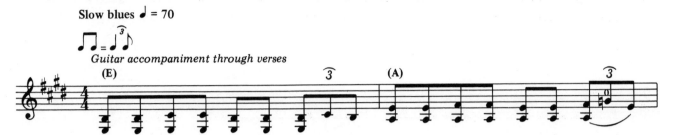

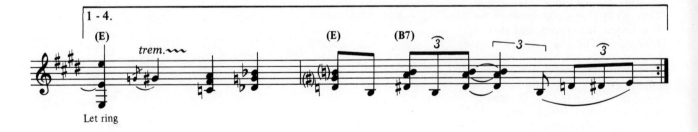

© Copyright 1975 & 1992 Eric Clapton.
All Rights Reserved. International Copyright Secured.

Verse 2:
I got mean things,
I got mean things all on my mind
Little girl, little girl
I got mean things all on my mind
Hate to leave you here, babe,
But you treat me so unkind.

Verse 3:
Runnin' down to the station,
Catch that old first mail train I see
Runnin' down to the station
Catch that old first mail train I see
I got the blues 'bout Miss So and So
And the child got the blues about me.

Verse 4:
And I'm leavin' this morning
With my arms folded up and cryin'
And I'm leavin' this morning
With my arms folded up and cryin'
I hate to leave my baby
But she treats me so unkind.

Verse 5:
I got mean things
I got mean things on my mind
I got mean things
I got mean things all on my mind
I got to leave my baby
But she treats me so unkind.

Ice Pick

Words & Music by Albert Collins.

4/4 Rhythm/Blues with embellishments
See Course Book No. 4 Pages 16-22

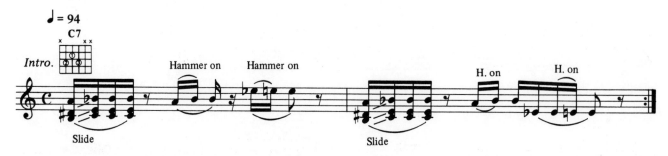

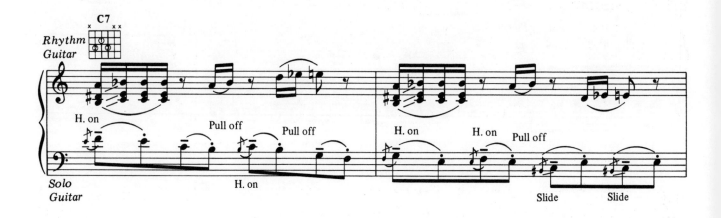

© Copyright 1978 Eyeball Music, USA.
Team Sonet Publishing Limited, 78 Stanley Gardens, London W3.
All Rights Reserved. International Copyright Secured.

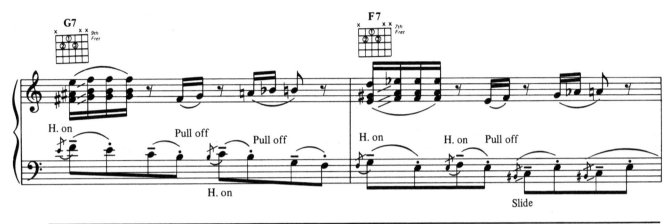

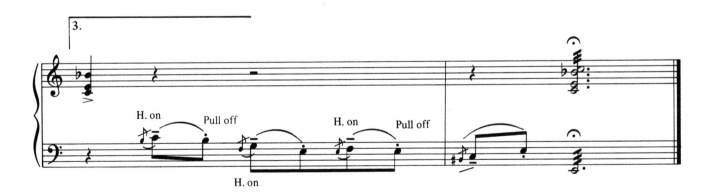

Worried About My Baby

Words & Music by Chester Burnette.

4/4 Rhythm/Blues figures with damping and embellishments
See Course Book No. 4 Page 11

Guitar accompaniment through Verses

© Copyright 1971 Arc Music Corporation, USA.
Tristan Music Limited, 22 Denmark Street, London WC2.
All Rights Reserved. International Copyright Secured.

Love you here ba - by what you tryin' - a - do tryin'- a - love me and a - a -

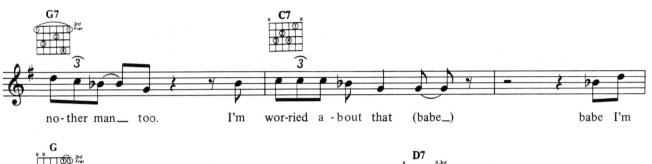

no - ther man_ too. I'm wor-ried a -bout that (babe_) babe I'm

wor-ried a - bout that And babe I'm wor-ried a -bout it ba - by and

Repeat for Verses and Solos

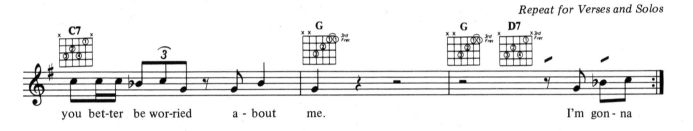

you bet-ter be wor-ried a - bout me. I'm gon - na

Verse 2:
I'm gonna take this time and I'm gonna say no more
And next time I tell you I'm gonna let you go
'Cos I'm worried about you
Babe I'm worried about you
Babe I'm worried about you baby
And you better be worried about me.

Verse 3:
Run here baby, sit on my knee
I've got something to tell you it's been worrying me
I'm worried about you
Babe I'm worried about you
Babe I'm worried about you baby
And you better be worried about me.

Verse 4:
Got up this morning, feeling bad,
Nobody knows how much trouble I've had
I'm worried about you
Babe I'm worried about you
Babe I'm worried about you baby,
And you better be worried about me.

Hideaway

Words & Music by Freddie King & Sonny Thompson.

4/4 Rhythm/Blues solo
See Course Book No. 4

♩ = 132

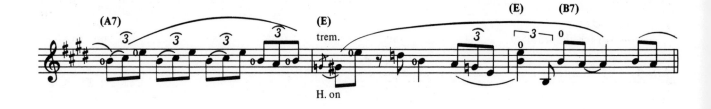

© Copyright 1961 Fort Knox Music Company Incorporated, USA.
Lark Music Limited, Iron Bridge House, 3 Bridge Approach,
London NW1.
All Rights Reserved. International Copyright Secured.

Hoochie Coochie Man

Words & Music by Willie Dixon.

4/4 Rhythm/Damped downstrokes/Triplet feel
See Course Book No. 4 Pages 11 & 24

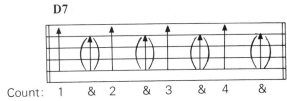

Slow blues ♩ = 72

© Copyright Arc Music Corporation, USA.
Jewel Music Publishing Company Limited, 129 Park Street,
London W1.
All Rights Reserved. International Copyright Secured.

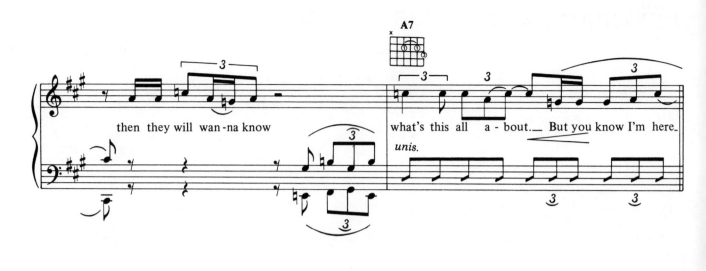

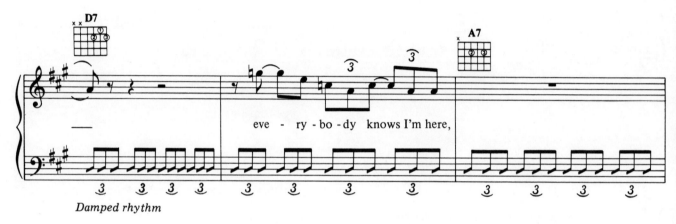

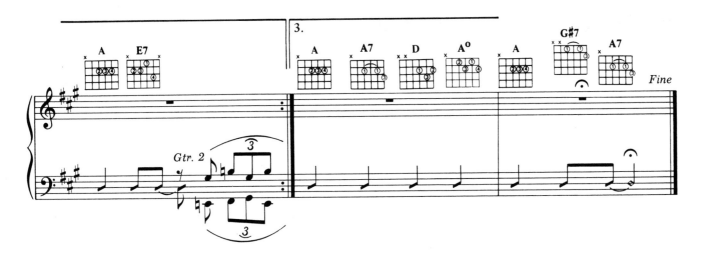

Verse 2:
I gotta black cat bone
I gotta a mojo too.
I got the time to conkeroo.
I'm gonna mess with you.
I'm gonna make you girls,
Lead me by my hand
Then the world'll know
The Hoochie Coochie Man.

But you know I'm here
Everybody knows I'm here
Well you know I'm a Hoochie Coochie Man
Everybody knows I'm here.

Verse 3:
On the seventh hour
On the seventh day
On the seventh month
The seven doctors say.
He was born for good luck
And that you'll see
I got seven hundred dollars
And don't you mess with me.

But you know I'm here
Everybody knows I'm here
Well you know I'm a Hoochie Coochie Man
Everybody knows I'm here.

So Many Roads, So Many Trains

Words & Music by Otis Rush.

4/4 Rhythm/Damped downstrokes
See Course Book No. 4 Pages 11 & 17

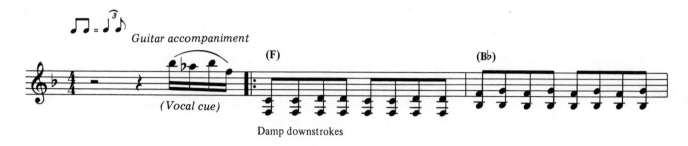

Guitar accompaniment

(Vocal cue)

Damp downstrokes

1, 2.

3.

Let ring

© Copyright Arc Music Corporation, USA.
Jewel Music Publishing Company Limited, 129 Park Street,
London W1.
All Rights Reserved. International Copyright Secured.

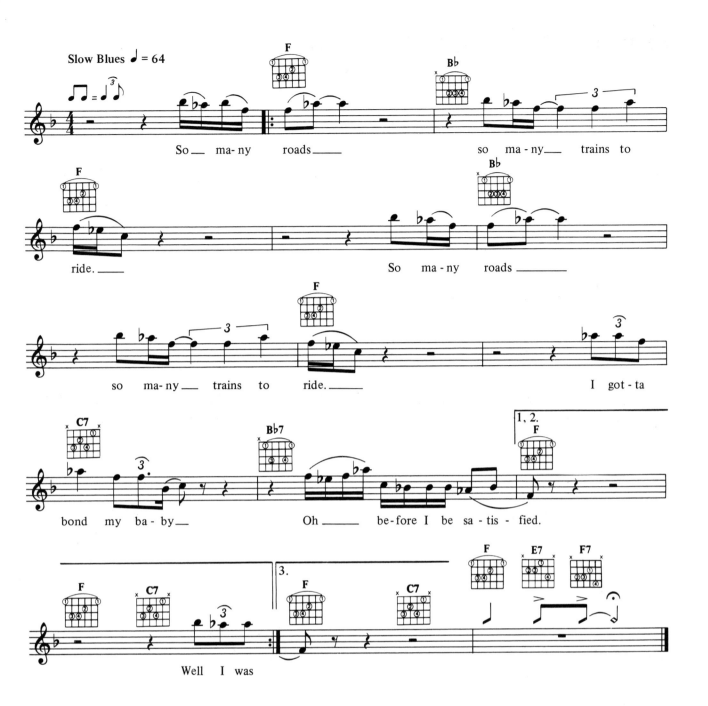

Slow Blues ♩ = 64

So ma-ny roads___ so ma-ny___ trains to ride.___ So ma-ny roads _____ so ma-ny___ trains to ride.___ I got-ta bond my ba-by___ Oh _____ be-fore I be sa-tis-fied. Well I was

Verse 2:
Well I was standing at my window
When I heard that whistle blow.
Oh, I was standing at my window
When I heard that whistle blow.
Yes it shone like a street light
Oh, oh but it wasn't me aboard.

Verse 3:
It was a big old barman
And a cruel engineer.
Oh, mean old barman
And a cruel old engineer.
Yeh, it's taken my baby
Yes, left me standing here.

Rollin' And Tumblin'

Words & Music by Muddy Waters.

4/4 Rhythm/Blues riff accompaniment
See Course Book No. 4 Pages 24-30

Guitar

© Copyright Arc Music Corporation, USA.
Jewel Music Publishing Company Limited, 129 Park Street,
London W1.
All Rights Reserved. International Copyright Secured.

Roll- in' and tumb -lin' — cried the whole night long.___

We were roll - in' and tumb-lin' —

cried — the whole night long.___ When I

To Coda ⊕ |1,2.

woke up this morn -ing all I had was gone. __

1^O *Guitar only* |3.
2^O *Vocal*   *Repeat ad lib. for Solos*   *To:*

We were out.

D.%. al Coda
(with repeats)   ⊕ *CODA*

Verse 3:
Well I love my baby
She's going to jump and shout
Well I love my baby
She's going to jump and shout
When her train rolls up boys
Gotta come walkin' on out.

Verse 4 on %.
When I cried last night mama,
I cried the night before.
When I cried last night mama,
I cried the night before.
When I hurt your feelings baby
You don't love me no more.

Verse 5:
As verse 1

The Beatles

Enya

Phil Collins

Van Morrison

Bob Dylan

Sting

Paul Simon

Tracy Chapman

Eric Clapton

Pink Floyd

New Kids On The Block

Bryan Adams

Tina Turner

Elton John

Bee Gees

Whitney Houston

AC/DC

Bringing you the words

All the latest in rock and pop. Plus the brightest and best in West End show scores. Music books for every instrument under the sun. And exciting new teach-yourself ideas like "Let's Play Keyboard" - in cassette/book packs, or on video. Available from all good music shops.

and music

Music Sales' complete catalogue lists thousands of titles and is available free from your local music shop, or direct from Music Sales Limited. Please send a cheque or postal order for £1.50 (for postage) to:

Music Sales Limited
Newmarket Road,
Bury St Edmunds,
Suffolk IP33 3YB

Buddy

Five Guys Named Moe

Les Misérables

West Side Story

Phantom Of The Opera

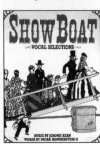
Show Boat

The Rocky Horror Show

Bringing you the world's best music.